汉语桥－中学生夏令营
Chinese Bridge Summer Camp for Foreign Students

中国欢迎你 短期汉语系列教材
Welcome to China

MW00762822

Xue Wushu

学武术
Martial Arts

才艺类

高等教育出版社·北京
HIGHER EDUCATION PRESS   BEIJING

"中国欢迎你"短期汉语系列教材

总策划　许　琳

总监制　王永利

策　划　陈　默　　邵亦鹏

监　制　薛　佼

编委会成员（按姓名音序排列）

常　春	迟兰英	代凝慧	丁　磊	丁　颖	董　赟
范祖奎	冯丽君	郝永宁	贺红梅	侯晓彬	纪仁盛
贾静芳	贾腾飞	姜志琪	金飞飞	鞠　慧	孔庆国
孔雪晴	李红艳	李　娜	梁小岸	梁　云	刘芳珍
刘玉波	卢小燕	罗来莉	罗兴平	孟宪滨	秦晓燕
屠晓蓓	汪正才	王　岱	王文龙	王　艳	王　瑜
王玉静	温　培	吴玉为	席忠祥	许　娟	杨　硕
杨晓霞	袁　勇	张　蕾	张　丽	张全生	张新江
张　勇	章新拓	赵江民	郑　颖	周　芳	周　荧
朱　璇	朱　芸				

　　随着中国与世界各国距离的拉近，越来越多的人渴望了解中国、体验中国。为了帮助"汉语桥"夏令营中小学生以及所有对中国感兴趣的外国朋友在较短时间内了解中国的语言和文化、历史与风俗，中国国家汉办/孔子学院总部组织研发了"中国欢迎你"短期汉语系列教材。

◉ 适用对象

　　本系列教材主要适用于来华参加夏令营的海外中小学生，也可用于海外孔子学院和孔子课堂作为汉语教学辅助资源。

◉ 教材构成

　　本系列教材分为三大类：语言类、才艺类和地域类。

　　《学武术》是才艺类教材中的一册，主要内容包括中国武术介绍，涉及武术门派、兵器、抱拳礼、基本动作等知识，同时提供了金刚拳和功夫扇两套易学易练的武术套路示范。本书将文化与才艺学习有机地结合起来，同时配以丰富的练习和活动，目的在于帮助学习者在较短时间内了解中国武术的基本知识，掌握基本的武术动作和武术套路。本书的参考教学时间为6～8学时。

◉ 编写特色

　　1. 全新的编写理念：本系列教材借鉴了全新的外语教学理念和最先进的外语教学法成果，真正做到以学习者为中心，满足学习者的个性化需求。

　　2. 全新的编写风格：本系列教材话题实用，内容简单，形式丰富，图文并茂，寓教于乐，注重实效，目的在于使汉语变得"易懂、易学、易用"。

　　3. 全新的教学设计：本系列教材以任务和活动为主线，便于教师进行教学设计，充分调动学习者的兴趣，实现轻松有效的课堂教学。

　　让我们翻开书，一起去感知充满魅力的汉语和中国文化！

编委会

2011年5月

Contents 目 录

Martial 武
Arts 术

Introduction to Martial Arts 武术介绍

Martial arts originated in primitive societies. Over thousands of years, people accumulated diverse skills of attack, defense and combat for self-defense, obtaining food or competing for wealth and power, and invented various weapons. As civilization progressed, martial arts became less aggressive and developed into a sport.

　　武术的起源可以追溯到原始社会。在几千年的历史中，人类为了自卫、获取食物，或是争夺财富和权力，逐渐积累了攻防、格斗的技能，并发明了各种兵器。随着社会文明的不断进步，武术的攻击性日益减弱，现在已发展成为一项体育运动。

Chinese martial arts emphasize the "integration of the internal and the external." The "internal" refers to a person's mental activities and the motion of one's breath, while the "external" means the physical movements of one's hands, eyes, body and footwork. Most of the true practitioners of martial arts pay attention to "*wu de*," the virtues of martial arts, which are to be patient and to promote justice. This is the so-called "great swordsman – for country and people." Chinese martial arts are popular among regular people. There are many masters in the rural areas or other lesser-known places. If one day you come across a grey-haired elderly person with a healthy complexion, walking quickly and steadily, it might just be that he or she is a real master of martial arts!

中华武术强调"内外合一"，"内"指内心活动和气息运行，"外"指手、眼、身法、脚步等外在的形体动作。真正的习武之人大都重视"武德"，戒急用忍，弘扬正义，所谓"侠之大者，为国为民"。中华武术普及于百姓之中，乡野间卧虎藏龙。如果你哪天看到一位鹤发童颜、健步如飞的老者，说不定他就是一位武术高人呢！

🔍 True or False? 判断正误

1. As society develops, martial arts become more aggressive.
   随着社会的发展，武术的攻击性越来越强。　　　　　（　　）

2. The "integration of the internal and the external" found in Chinese martial arts means the coordination of the spirit and body.
   中国武术的"内外合一"指的是精神和身体的配合。　（　　）

3. For true practitioners of martial arts, "*wu de*," the virtues of martial arts, is of vital importance.
   对习武者来说，"武德"是非常重要的。　　　　　　（　　）

| 形意拳 *Xingyi Quan* | | 太极拳 *Taiji Quan* |
| 八卦掌 *Bagua Zhang* | 南拳 *Nan Quan* | 咏春拳 *Yongchun Quan* |

There are many schools or factions of Chinese martial arts, and they present a truly splendid sight. In terms of geographical areas, there is "*Bei Tui*," the school north of the Yellow River and "*Nan Quan*," the school south of the Yellow River. Famous schools include the Shaolin School, the Wudang School, and the Emei School, etc. There are sometimes even further divisions inside the schools – if one section of a school develops a certain characteristic of its own, this section may grow into a new school. Large and small sects of the martial arts are just like a starry sky, creating a Chinese martial arts culture that has a long history and world-renowned reputation.

中国武术门派和套路众多，蔚为大观。按地域划分，黄河以北的为北派，素有"北腿"之称，黄河以南的为南派，以"南拳"闻名。比较有名的门派有少林派、武当派、峨眉派等。这些大派内部又有许多支派，各支派中的某一套路如果有显著特色，又可能发展成为新的支派。大大小小的武术派别犹如满天繁星，形成了历史悠久、名扬天下的中华武术文化。

🌀 Try It Yourself　试一试

Under the guidance of your instructor, learn some of the poses represented in the pictures above. Try to imitate these gestures and see who can do it the best.

在老师的指导下，简单了解本页上方的图片中几种有代表性的拳术。试着模仿图中的动作，看谁模仿得最好。

Weapons 兵器

Practice using weapons is an important part of learning martial arts. There have been countless kinds of weapons throughout history, ranging from huge iron hammers to small needles. Both of these, for example, were used as weapons in martial arts. There is an ancient Chinese saying that says one should: "Be versatile and be good at all of 18 weapons." In this saying, the number "18" is a general number to mean "several weapons" – there are many more weapons than eighteen. As time goes on, most weapons become obsolete. Only a few, such as knives, spears, swords, sticks, and whips are still used today.

学练器械是习武的重要部分。中国历史上出现过的武术器械种类不计其数，大到铁锤，小到绣花针，都曾是武术器械中的一员，中国古代有句俗语说"十八般武艺，样样精通"，这里的"十八"不过是泛称而已，实际上的武术器械远不止此数。随着时代的发展，大多数武术器械已被淘汰，只有刀、枪、剑、棍、九节鞭等保留了下来。

 Let's Think 想一想

Try to classify the weapons in the pictures on page 5.

试着给第5页图中的兵器分类。

Long weapons 长兵器：   (   ) (   )
Short weapons 短兵器：   (   ) (   )
"Soft" weapons 软兵器：   (   ) (   )

① 单刀	② 棍	③ 剑	④ 双节棍	⑤ 花枪	⑥ 九节鞭
dāndāo	gùn	jiàn	shuāngjiégùn	huāqiāng	jiǔjiébiān
Short-hilted broadsword	Stick	Sword	Nunchakus	Spear	Whip

Fist-wrapping Salute
抱拳礼

The fist-wrapping salute is a special way for martial arts practitioners to greet each other. The specific gesture is to stretch both arms parallel to the ground with the elbows toward the outside. The palm of the left hand is stretched out and the right hand forms a fist. The palm of the left hand touches the top of the right hand and both hands are pushed forward slightly.

　　抱拳礼是习武者见面行礼的特殊方式，其做法是两臂平伸与地面平行，肘尖向外，左手成掌，右手成拳，左掌搭在右拳上，向前一推。

💡 Let's Think 想一想

What is the difference between Po's gesture in the picture and the gesture of the man above? Do you know what Po's gesture means?

阿宝的抱拳礼和上图有什么不同？你知道阿宝的这个姿势代表什么意思吗？

⛽ Chinese Learning 汉语加油站

▶ 师傅领进门，修行在个人。
Shī fu lǐng jìn mén, xiū xíng zài gè rén.
The master teaches the trade, but the apprentice's skill is self-made.

▶ 冬练三九，夏练三伏。
Dōng liàn sān jiǔ, xià liàn sān fú.
Train either in the coldest time in winter or in the hottest time in summer.

▶ 外练筋骨皮，内练一口气。
Wài liàn jīn gǔ pí, nèi liàn yì kǒu qì.
Train your body both internally and externally.

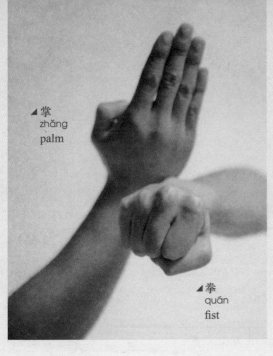

掌
zhǎng
palm

Basic Hand Gestures and Footwork
基本手型和步型

拳
quán
fist

弓 步
gōng bù
bow stance

虚 步
xū bù
tiptoe stance

马 步
mǎ bù
horse-riding stance

歇 步
xiē bù
resting stance

仆 步
pú bù
drop stance

Activity 课堂活动

Learn to sing a song about Chinese kung fu.　在老师的带领下，学唱一段关于中国功夫的歌曲吧。

卧似一张弓，　站似一棵松。
wò sì yì zhāng gōng　zhàn sì yì kē sōng

不动不摇坐如钟，　走路一阵风。
bú dòng bù yáo zuò rú zhōng　zǒu lù yí zhèn fēng

南拳和北腿，　少林武当功。
nán quán hé běi tuǐ　shāo lín wǔ dāng gōng

太极八卦连环掌，　中华有神功。
tài jí bā guà lián huán zhǎng　zhōng huá yǒu shén gōng

Lyrics 歌词

Lying like a bow,　卧似一张弓，

Standing like a pine tree,　站似一棵松，

Sitting steadily as a clock,　不动不摇坐如钟，

Walking as swiftly as the wind.　走路一阵风。

Nan Quan and *Bei Tui*,　南拳和北腿，

the kung fu of *Shaolin* and *Wudang*,　少林武当功，

Taiji, *Bagua* and *Lianhuan Zhang*,　太极八卦连环掌，

China boasts of her miracles.　中华有神功。

King Kong Boxing 金刚拳套路

"King Kong," in Buddhism, refers to Buddha's attendant wrestlers. They hold instruments made of gold, silver, copper, iron, and other materials. They are gigantic in stature and extremely powerful. King Kong boxing is a branch of Shaolin kung fu. This set of King Kong Boxing is a selection from the easy, practical, and classical moves of traditional King Kong Boxing routines. It inherited Shaolin kung fu's characteristics of integrating softness and hardness and it is ideal for beginners to learn.

金刚，在佛教中指的是佛的侍从力士，他们手拿用金、银、铜、铁等材料做成的法器，身体巨大有力。金刚拳是少林拳的一个分支。这套金刚拳是在传统金刚拳套路中精心挑选的实用性强、简单易学的经典动作，继承了少林拳朴实无华、刚柔相济的特点，非常适合武术初学者学习。

1 预备式 yù bèi shì
Opening position

2 起势 qǐ shì
Starting movement

Knowledge Links 知识链接

Shaolin kung fu has a distinctive feature in its training, which is the sound cheer. Practitioners will normally produce a sound with the last action at the end of a set of exercises. There are also various sounds like "ah," "woo," and "ha" during the training process. These sounds come from the abdominal cavity. They are short, powerful, and have a shocking effect.

少林拳在演练过程中有一个特点，就是以声助威。演练者通常会在套路结尾时随最后的动作发声助威，演练过程中也常有"呀"、"呜"、"哈"等不同的发声。这些发声源自腹腔，短促有力，富有震撼力。

3 左格冲心拳
zuǒ gé chōng xīn quán
Block left and strike the heart

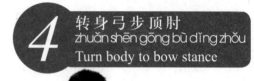

4 转身弓步顶肘
zhuǎn shēn gōng bù dǐng zhǒu
Turn body to bow stance

5 弓步挑掌
gōng bù tiǎo zhǎng
Jab palm in bow stance

6 提膝探爪
tí xī tàn zhuǎ
Raise left knee to stretch claws

7 击手炮
jī shǒu pào
Strike hands

8 上架马步冲拳
shàng jià mǎ bù chōng quán
Block and thrust fist in horse-riding stance

9 上架马步冲拳
shàng jià mǎ bù chōng quán
Block and thrust fist in horse-riding stance

10 弓步后栽拳
gōng bù hòu zāi quán
Thrust fist backward in bow stance

11 弓步砍掌
gōng bù kǎn zhǎng
Cut palm in bow stance

12 独立双劈拳
dú lì shuāng pī quán
Hammer both fists with raised knee

13 马步架拳
mǎ bù jià quán
Circle arms in horse-riding stance

14 还原
huán yuán
Closing movement

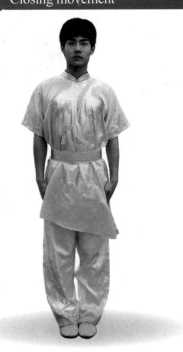

Detailed Explanation of the Moves in King Kong Boxing
金刚拳动作详解

1. Opening position
预备式

Stand straight with the feet together, arms and hands hanging down naturally at the sides of the body. Look straight ahead.

两脚并步站立，两手自然下垂，头正身直，两眼平视前方。

2. Starting movement
起势

Take one small step left with your left foot, and toes stay firmly on the ground. Feet should be about shoulder-width apart. Make two fists and bring them to the sides of your waist, the front of the fists facing up. Keep your back straight and hold your stomach in. Then, turn your head to the left and look in that direction.

左脚向左跨小半步，脚趾抓地，双脚与肩同宽。双手握拳，拳心朝上抱于腰间，挺胸收腹，头左摆，目视左方。

3. Block left and strike the heart
左格冲心拳

Take another step left with your left foot to form a low horse-riding stance. Raise your left arm upwards, toward the left as if to block a blow from that direction. Have the back of your fist facing up and your eyes looking left. Turn left 90 degrees to form a left bow stance. Withdraw the left fist back to your waist, the front of the fist facing upward. Simultaneously and powerfully punch the right fist forward with the front of the fist facing downwards. The right arm should be level with the shoulder. Look straight ahead.

左脚向左跨一步成马步，左小臂左上格出，拳面朝上，目视左方。身体左转90°成左弓步，收左拳与腰间，拳心朝上，右拳拳心朝下向前冲出，右臂与肩平，力达拳面，目视前方。

4. Turn body to bow stance
转身弓步顶肘

Turn right 180 degrees to form a right bow stance. At the same time, unfold the left fist and press the palm upon the front of the right fist. Bend the right arm and thrust backwards, using strength to strike with the elbow. Look straight ahead.

身体右转180°成右弓步，同时，左拳变掌紧贴右拳面，屈右肘向后顶，力达右肘，目视前方。

5. Jab palm in bow stance
弓步挑掌

Turn left 180 degrees to form left bow stance. Thrust the left hand upward, and withdraw the right fist to waist-level.

身体左转180°成左弓步，左掌经体前由下至前撩出上挑，右拳拳心朝上抱于腰间。

6. Raise left knee to stretch claws
提膝探爪

Turn right 180 degrees and use your right foot to step forward. Meanwhile, open your right hand into a tiger claw and stretch low to the right. At the same time, raise your left knee and withdraw the left fist to waist-level. Look at your right hand.

身体右转180°，右脚向前上步，右拳变虎爪向右下探出。左腿提膝绷脚面扣于右膝前。左掌变拳放于腰间，目视右手。

7. Strike hands
击手炮

Squat down and stamp the ground with both feet side by side. Use your right fist to strike your left palm. Look straight forward.

双脚相并，震地屈膝半蹲，右爪变拳拳心朝上，左拳变掌掌指朝下相击于膝前，目视前方。

8. Block and thrust fist in horse-riding stance
上架马步冲拳

Turn right. Step forward with your left foot to form the horse-riding stance. At the same time, the right arm blocks up and stays one fist-length above the head, with the left fist thrust leftward.

身体右转，左脚向左上步成马步。同时，右臂经体前向上架于头顶上方一立拳高，拳心朝上，左掌变拳向左冲出，力达拳面。

9. Block and thrust fist in horse-riding stance
上架马步冲拳

Turn left 180 degrees. Step backward with your left foot to form the horse-riding stance. At the same time, your left arm blocks up and stays one fist-length above the head, with your right fist thrust rightward.

身体左转180°，左脚向左撤步成马步。同时，左拳向上架于头顶上方一立拳高，拳心朝上，右拳落于腰间后向右冲出，力达拳面。

10. Thrust fist backward in bow stance
弓步后栽拳

Turn right 180 degrees. Step backward with your right foot to form the bow stance. At the same time, thrust your left fist backward, with your right elbow held up to the right.

身体右转180°，右脚向右撤步成弓步。右臂屈肘向前上方顶出，拳背停于太阳穴处。同时，左拳内旋贴身体左侧，向后下方冲出。

11. Cut palm in bow stance
弓步砍掌

Turn left 90 degrees, and withdraw your left foot. Then step forward to form the bow stance. At the same time, your right palm cuts in front to the right, to be level with your ears. Look at your right palm.

身体左转90°，左脚收回后向前上步成左弓步。同时，左手变掌外旋，掌心朝上向右前方砍出，力达小指侧，高与耳平，目视右掌。

12. Hammer both fists with raised knee
独立双劈拳

Lift your right knee, and cross your arms in front of your chest. Brandish both fists and curve them out to the shoulder level.

提右膝绷脚面扣于左膝前，双手握拳交叉于体前，右手在外，双手经头顶上方向外绕圆，向两侧下砸，拳眼朝上，高与肩平。

13. Circle arms in horse-riding stance
马步架拳

After your right foot lands, take a step to the left with your left foot to form the horse-riding stance. At the same time, place your left fist on top of your left knee. The right fist rests on top of your head, the front of the fist facing upward.

右脚落地，左脚向左跨一步成马步，同时，左拳放在左膝盖上方，拳心向后。右手握拳，拳心朝上架于头顶。

14. Closing movement
还原

Both fists open into palms and fall slowly and naturally. The shoulder and bottom relax. Slowly take three breaths.

双手变掌自然下垂，肩部、臀部放松下沉。用鼻孔均匀呼吸三次。

Kung Fu Fan 功夫扇套路

A fan is both a daily necessity and a kind of martial arts weapon. This set of movements with fan have absorbed the essence of traditional Chinese martial arts, bringing together a combination of fan waving with the flexible offensive and defensive techniques of martial arts. It integrates hardness and softness, is vivid in shape and spirit, and also helps to stretch the joints and regulate the flow of vital energy.

扇子既是生活用品，又是武术器械的一种。此套功夫扇吸取了中华传统武术的精华，使扇子的挥舞与武术的攻防技术巧妙结合，刚柔相济，形神兼备，舒筋理气。

1 预备式
yù bèi shì
Opening position

2 并步抱扇
bìng bù bào shān
Hold the fan at attention

4 弓步刺扇
gōng bù cì shān
Jab with fan in bow stance

3 马步格扇
mǎ bù gé shān
Parry fan in horse-riding stance

5 回身架掌劈扇
huí shēn jiǎ zhǎng pī shàn
Thrust with hand and chop with fan in bow stance

6 弓步开扇
gōng bù kāi shàn
Open fan in bow stance

7 高虚步合扇
gāo xū bù hé shàn
Close fan in high tiptoe stance

8 马步刺扇
mǎ bù cì shàn
Jab fan in horse-riding stance

9 并步砸拳
bìng bù zá quán
Strike foot and hammer fist

10 下蹲转身扫扇
xià dūn zhuǎn shēn sǎo shàn
Squat and sweep fan with the body turned back

11 右弓步刺扇
yòu gōng bù cì shàn
Jab with fan in right bow stance

12 右弓步开扇
yòu gōng bù kāi shàn
Open fan in right bow stance

13 歇步云抱扇
xiē bù yún bào shàn
Clouds and hold fan in resting stance

14 提膝抱扇
tí xī bào shàn
Hold fan and lift knee

15 垫步左弓步刺扇
diàn bù zuǒ gōng bù cì shàn
Jab fan in left bow stance

16 插步后击扇
chā bù hòu jī shàn
Jab fan back in a cross stance

17 插步开扇
chā bù kāi shān
Open fan in a cross stance

18 转身云扇
zhuǎn shēn yún shān
Clouds with fan and turn back

19 直身抱扇
zhí shēn bào shān
Hold the fan and stand up

20 收式
shōu shì
Finish

Detailed Explanation of the Moves in Kungfu Fan
功夫扇动作详解

1. Opening position
预备式

Stand at attention, holding the fan with your right hand. Look forward.

并步直立，右手持扇，目视前方。

2. Hold the fan at attention
并步抱扇

Standing at attention, hold the fan with palms up. Look forward.

并步直立，立掌抱扇，目视前方。

3. Parry fan in horse-riding stance
马步格扇

Step your left foot to the left and bend your knees. Parry both hands to each side. Direct the force into your forearm, and look to the left.

左脚开步，屈膝马步。两臂下落，体侧格挡，力达前臂，目视左前。

4. Jab with fan in bow stance
弓步刺扇

Turn left 90 degrees. Jab with the fan in bow stance, keeping the arm level with the shoulder. Look forward.

向左转身，弓步刺扇，臂与肩平，目视前方。

5. Thrust with hand and chop with fan in bow stance
回身架掌劈扇

Turn right to form a right bow stance. Use your right hand to chop with the fan backward, keeping your arm level with the shoulder. Look forward.

向右转身，成右弓步。右手抡劈，臂与肩平，目视前方。

6. Open fan in bow stance
弓步开扇

Hold the last pose and open the fan. Look forward.

保持上式，抖腕开扇，目视前方。

7. Close fan in high tiptoe stance
高虚步合扇

Balance your weight back, then draw the fan back to your waist in a high tiptoe stance. Look forward.

重心后移，起身站立，成高虚步，持扇腰间，目视前方。

8. Jab fan in horse-riding stance
马步刺扇

Turn left into a horse-riding stance, at the same time use your right hand to jab with the fan at shoulder-level. Look to the right.

向左转身，屈膝马步，右手刺扇，臂与肩平，目视右方。

9. Strike foot and hammer fist
并步砸拳

Take your right foot, move it to the left and squat. At the same time, hold the fan and strike, with the fan-side face forward.

右脚左收，屈膝并步，持扇砸拳，扇尖向前。

10. Squat and sweep fan with the body turned back
下蹲转身扫扇

Step backward with your right foot. Hold the fan in your right hand and sweep it back quickly.

右后撤步，右臂伸展，猛力后扫。

11. Jab with fan in right bow stance
右弓步刺扇

Stand. Take your right foot and step forward into a right bow stance. Using the right hand, chop with the fan at shoulder-height. Look forward.

起身直立，右脚上步成右弓步，右手刺扇，臂与肩平，目视前方。

12. Open fan in right bow stance
右弓步开扇

Hold the last pose and open the fan horizontally.

保持上式，抖腕开扇，扇沿朝前。

13. Clouds and hold fan in resting stance
歇步云抱扇

Take your right foot, step backward and squat. Perform clouds with fan upward and then hold the fan forward. Look forward.

右脚撤步，头顶云扇，蹲成歇步，持扇抱于胸前，目视前方。

14. Hold fan and lift knee
提膝抱扇

Take your right foot and step forward. Lift the left knee and draw the fan back to the waist. Look forward.

起身直立，右脚迈步，提起左膝，收扇腰间，目视左前。

15. Jab fan in left bow stance
垫步左弓步刺扇

Take a step forward. Jump forward into a left bow stance. At the same time, chop with the fan, level with the shoulder.

左脚上步，催步前跳成左弓步，右手刺扇，臂与肩平。

16. Jab fan back in a cross stance
插步后击扇

Take your left foot back. Jab the fan down toward the back, level with the shoulder. Look at the fan. At the same time, use your left hand to parry left with the palm in the center, facing forward.

左脚后撤，翻手后击，扇与肩平，目视扇尖。同时，左手上格，掌心朝前。

17. Open fan in a cross stance
插步开扇

Hold the last pose and open the fan.

保持上式，抖腕开扇。

18. Clouds with fan and turn back
转身云扇

Turn your right hand down, with the right arm straight, and move it down and back. Turn the left hand forward, then left 180 degrees. Move the right hand to the left. Turn the left hand down and revolve it. At the same time, use your right hand to make clouds with the fan facing up and circling.

右掌下翻，右臂伸直，左掌向下，落至胸前。左转180°，重心左移，左掌下翻旋转，同时，右手至头顶，翻转360°平云。

19. Hold the fan and stand up
直身抱扇

Take your right foot and move left. Hold the fan forward with the body upright. Look forward.

右脚左迈，身体直立，落扇胸前，目视前方。

20. Finish
收式

Take your left foot and step right in the closing stance. At the same time, use your right hand to close the fan. Then hold the fan in the left hand. Stand up straight and face forward.

左脚向右成并步。同时，右手胸前合扇，左手接扇，还原直立。

Answers 答案

True or False? 判断正误

1. (F)   2. (F)   3. (T)

 Let's Think 想一想

Long weapons: ⑤Spear   ②Stick

长兵器：⑤花枪   ②棍

Short weapons: ①Short-hilted broadsword   ③Sword

短兵器：①单刀   ③剑

"Soft" weapons: ④Nunchakus   ⑥Whip

软兵器：④双节棍   ⑥九节鞭

 Let's Think 想一想

For the hand-clasping gesture in the picture, the palm of the left hand spreads and the right hand makes a fist. Po's hand-clasping gesture is made by the left hand as a fist and the right hand stretching. This gesture of Po seems provocative, as if asking for a fight.

图片中的抱拳礼左掌右拳，阿宝的抱拳礼是左拳右掌。图片中阿宝的这个姿势有挑衅的意思。

图书在版编目（CIP）数据

学武术 / 国家汉办 / 孔子学院总部编著 . —北京：高等教育出版
社，2011.6（2013.1 重印）

《中国欢迎你》短期汉语系列教材 . 才艺类

ISBN 978-7-04-032803-5

Ⅰ.①学…　Ⅱ.①国…　Ⅲ.①汉语—阅读教学—对外汉语教学
—教学参考资料　Ⅳ.① H195.4

中国版本图书馆 CIP 数据核字（2011）第 101728 号

| 策划编辑 | 周　芳 | 责任编辑 | 鞠　慧 | 封面设计 | 乔　剑 | 版式设计 | 悦尔视觉 |
| 插图选配 | 鞠　慧 | 责任校对 | 鞠　慧 李　桑 | 责任印制 | 朱学忠 | | |

出版发行	高等教育出版社	咨询电话	400-810-0598
社　　址	北京市西城区德外大街4号	网　　址	http://www.hep.edu.cn
邮政编码	100120		http://www.hep.com.cn
印　　刷	北京信彩瑞禾印刷厂	网上订购	http://www.landraco.com
开　　本	787×1092 1/16		http://www.landraco.com.cn
印　　张	1.75	版　　次	2011 年 6 月第 1 版
字　　数	44 000	印　　次	2013 年 1 月第 3 次印刷
购书热线	010-58581118	定　　价	13.80元